A Little Green Monster

Written by Jeanne Willis

Illustrated by Richard Watson

A little green monster comes along,
bright flowers in his hair.
A little green monster comes along.
What will he do there?

He is growling.
Growl! Growl! Growl!
He is howling.
Howl! Howl! Howl!

A little green monster comes along.
He's looking for a lair.
A little green monster comes along.
What will he do there?

He is crashing.
Crash! Crash! Crash!
He is thrashing.
Thrash! Thrash! Thrash!

A little green monster comes along.
He's jumping on a chair.

A little green monster comes along.
What will he do there?

He is jumping.
Jump! Jump! Jump!
He is thumping.
Thump! Thump! Thump!

A little green monster comes along.
He's marching up the stairs.

A little green monster comes along.
What will he do there?

He is floating.
Float! Float! Float!
He is boating.
Boat! Boat! Boat!

A little green monster comes along.
He sniffs and sniffs the air.

A little green monster comes along.
What will he do there?

He is munching.
Munch! Munch! Munch!

He is crunching.
Crunch! Crunch! Crunch!

A little green monster comes along.
Slurp! Slurp! Slurp!
"What will you do now?" I said.
And he said, "BURP!"